Bald and Bonkers Show

Bald and Bonkers Show

Episode Guide Part 1

Sara Larson

Dakota Frandsen, Christopher Moule

Bald and Bonkers Network LLC

This guide, titled "Bald and Bonkers Show: Season 1 Guide," is intended to serve as a companion piece to the show and is provided by Bald and Bonkers Network LLC for promotional purposes. By accessing this guide, you agree to the following terms:

1. **Marketing Strategy:** The information presented in this guide is part of a marketing strategy employed by Bald and Bonkers Show and Bald and Bonkers Network LLC to extend the show's reach. It is designed to enhance the viewer's understanding and enjoyment of the show.
2. **No Copyright Infringement Intended:** This guide does not intend to infringe upon any copyrights or intellectual property rights. All copyrighted materials, trademarks, and other proprietary information are the property of their respective owners. Any use of such materials in this guide is purely for illustrative and promotional purposes.
3. **Views Expressed by Guests and Hosts:** The views, opinions, and expressions presented by the guests and hosts of the Bald and Bonkers Show, whether in this guide or during the show itself, are strictly their own. These views do not necessarily reflect the opinions or positions of Bald and Bonkers Network LLC. Bald and Bonkers Network LLC disclaims any responsibility for the views expressed by individuals on the show.
4. **Accuracy of Information:** While efforts have been made to ensure the accuracy of the information presented in this guide, Bald and Bonkers Network LLC does not guarantee the completeness or accuracy of any information. Viewers are encouraged to verify details independently.
5. **Changes to the Show:** Bald and Bonkers Network LLC reserves the right to make changes to the Bald and Bonkers Show, including but not limited to the show format, schedule, and featured guests, without prior notice. This guide may not always reflect the most current information.

By accessing this guide, you acknowledge that you have read, understood, and agreed to the terms outlined in this legal disclaimer. If you do not agree with any part of these terms, you are advised not to use or rely on the information provided in this guide.

First Printing, 2024

ISBN: 979-8-8691-2235-3
EISBN: 979-8-8691-2236-0

How To Use This Guide

Introduction to the "Bald and Bonkers Show: Season 1 Guide"

Welcome to the captivating world of the "Bald and Bonkers Show: Season 1 Guide." This guide serves as your exclusive backstage pass, offering a glimpse into each episode of the Bald and Bonkers Show and the intriguing stories that unfold within.

1. ***Episode Overview:*** Delve into the essence of each episode as we provide a concise yet comprehensive overview. From supernatural phenomena to life's diverse facets, the Bald and Bonkers Show offers an array of topics that resonate with audiences of all backgrounds.

2. ***Guest Information:*** Get to know the fascinating individuals who grace the show with their presence. Our guide may include details such as guest websites, social media links, and items for sale. Please note that these details are shared for informational purposes and may not be directly endorsed by Bald and Bonkers Show or Bald and Bonkers Network LLC.

3. No Copyright Infringement Intended: We want to make it clear that our intention is not to infringe upon any copyrights or intellectual property rights. Information about guests, events, or merchandise not directly affiliated with Bald and Bonkers Show or Bald and Bonkers Network LLC is shared with utmost respect for the original creators.

4. Professionalism and Relationships: Certain relationships with past guests may have dissolved for reasons kept confidential out of respect and professionalism. Consequently, some episodes may not appear in this guide but will continue to be available through Bald and Bonkers Show distribution points.

5. Inclusive Vision: Hosts Christopher Moule and Dakota Frandsen have crafted the Bald and Bonkers Show as an open platform for individuals of all backgrounds to share their unique stories without prejudice. This inclusive vision extends to Bald and Bonkers Network LLC, where independent creatives are empowered to break the mold and turn their dreams into reality. While candid in their discussions, hosts openly address individuals and situations they perceive as operating with malice intent, which may lead to moments that challenge audience comfort.

6. Diverse Topics: Although the Bald and Bonkers Show predominantly explores supernatural themes, the hosts, Chris and Dakota, occasionally steer into other aspects of life. Expect the unexpected, as there truly is something for everyone on this exhilarating journey through the Bald and Bonkers universe.

Embark on this adventure with us as we unravel the mysteries, celebrate individual stories, and embrace the diverse tapestry of the Bald and Bonkers Show. Enjoy the guide, and let the journey begin!

Episodes

Episode 1 - The Premiere

Summary

The Bald and Bonkers Show addresses recent controversies, introduces upcoming episodes, and discusses strange news stories. They plan to release the show as a podcast and invite guests for future episodes.

Description

Christopher Moule and Dakota Frandsen join forces to bring you, "The Bald and Bonkers," where an unfiltered view into worlds known and unknown is brought to you with amazing guests and more! Attention: This show is designed to create a neutral environment for open discussions on all sorts of topics, paranormal and normal. As such some topics may be offensive to some viewers, so please if you feel you might be offended please do move on. Be sure to subscribe to the channel, hit the notification bell, as this will not only be aired on YouTube but be shared across anywhere you get your podcasts! Join the show live to maybe even join in on the fun and have your questions answered LIVE.

This week's guest: The Hosts! Get to know Dakota and Chris just a bit more and hear crazy news from around the globe!

Key Insights

- ◈ The Bald and Bonkers YouTube show is premiering with a live stream episode that addresses recent controversies and extends an olive branch to those affected.

- ◈ The hosts apologize and take responsibility for their actions, expressing a desire to move forward and work together with those involved in the controversy.

- ◈ The show plans to release future episodes as a podcast and expand distribution to reach a wider audience on platforms like Alexa, Google, and iTunes.

- ◈ The hosts discuss strange and funny news stories, such as the possibility of penguins being aliens and a possessed goat in India.

- ◈ They invite Lisa Fry for a panel discussion on ETs and consciousness, aiming to exchange ideas and continue their mission of exploring the paranormal.

- ◈ They tease upcoming episodes, including a short contact on UFOs and potential collaborations with other guests in the future.

- ◈ The hosts plan to have a Halloween episode where audience members can share their own supernatural stories and experiences.

Episode 2 - Living History Comes Alive

Summary

The video script is about a conversation between two hosts and their guest, Drew from "Living History Comes Alive." They discuss Drew's recent paranormal investigation and share personal experiences and plans for future investigations.

Description

This week's guest: Living History Comes Alive!

https://www.youtube.com/channel/UCnr-bzAJ2xQ6b7BNEBFHB-CQ

Christopher Moule and Dakota Frandsen join forces to bring you, "The Bald and Bonkers," where an unfiltered view into worlds known and unknown is brought to you with amazing guests and more! Attention: This show is designed to create a neutral environment for open discussions on all sorts of topics, paranormal and normal. As such some topics may be offensive to some viewers, so please if you feel you might be offended please do move on. Be sure to subscribe to the channel, hit the notification bell, as this will not only be aired on YouTube but be shared across anywhere you get your podcasts! Join the show live to maybe even join in on the fun and have your questions answered LIVE.

Key Insights

- ◈ Drew's personal near-death experience has made him more sensitive to paranormal activity and has influenced his investigations.
- ◈ The best evidence Drew has captured is a video of two mysterious eyes in a mausoleum, which skeptics have questioned but he believes to be genuine.
- ◈ Future investigations include haunted locations such as Prospect Hill and a haunted town called Goleen, offering potential for more paranormal encounters.
- ◈ Drew emphasizes the importance of obtaining permission and ensuring safety when conducting paranormal investigations, sharing his own experiences and cautionary tales.

Episode 3 - CONTACT - Episode 2 From the Asherz

Summary

The video script discusses various topics related to UFOs, paranormal activities, and social media platforms like Facebook and YouTube. It highlights the prevalence of fake content and the suppression of truth by mainstream media. The script also mentions upcoming guests and a charity event for Alzheimer's awareness.

Description

Christopher Moule and Dakota Frandsen join forces to bring you, "The Bald and Bonkers," where an unfiltered view into worlds known and unknown is brought to you with amazing guests and more! CONTACT is the show dedicated strictly to the UFO Disclosure Movements and more! You never quite know what will happen! Want to know where you can catch Bald and Bonkers? Check out this link: https://www.flowcode.com/page/baldand... Be sure to subscribe to the channel, hit the notification bell, as this will not only be aired on YouTube but be shared across anywhere you get your podcasts! Join the show live to maybe even join in on the fun and have your questions answered LIVE.

Key Insights

- [◈] The prevalence of fake content on social media

platforms like Facebook and YouTube raises questions about the suppression of truth and the influence of mainstream media.

- [🔮] The shift in NASA's focus to UFOs indicates a growing interest in the subject and the potential for more transparency in the future.
- [🔮] The vastness of the universe and the number of galaxies make it highly unlikely that Earth is the only planet with intelligent life.
- [🔮] The portrayal of paranormal activities and UFOs in mainstream media often exaggerates or distorts the truth for entertainment purposes.
- [🔮] Collaboration between paranormal investigators, mediums, and experts in various fields can lead to a better understanding of the paranormal and extraterrestrial phenomena.
- [⚠] The manipulation of social media algorithms and the prevalence of fake content have significant implications for public perception and the spread of misinformation.
- [🔮] The charity event for Alzheimer's awareness demonstrates the channel's commitment to using its platform for positive causes and making a difference in the world.

Episode 4 - Halloween Special

Summary

The video script revolves around a group of paranormal investigators discussing their beliefs about the afterlife and sharing personal experiences. They also discuss protection methods and the difference between demons and negative human spirits.

Description

This week's guest: A few paranormal people Christopher Moule and Dakota Frandsen join forces to bring you, "The Bald and Bonkers," where an unfiltered view into worlds known and unknown is brought to you with amazing guests and more! Attention: This show is designed to create a neutral environment for open discussions on all sorts of topics, paranormal and normal. As such some topics may be offensive to some viewers, so please if you feel you might be offended please do move on. Be sure to subscribe to the channel, hit the notification bell, as this will not only be aired on YouTube but be shared across anywhere you get your podcasts! Join the show live to maybe even join in on the fun and have your questions answered LIVE.

Key Insights

- ◈ The belief in the afterlife varies among the group,

with some believing in life everlasting and others in different realms after death.

- ◈ The distinction between demons and negative human spirits is made, with demons being non-human entities and twisted humans being angry and powerful spirits without control.

- ◈ Personal protection methods differ among the investigators, with some using crystals, oils, and prayers, while others rely on personal belongings and spiritual baths.

- ◈ The mindset and belief in one's own protection play a crucial role in paranormal investigations, as fear and vulnerability can attract negative energies.

- ◈ The presence of a protective spirit or guide can provide additional support and prevent harmful entities from approaching, but caution is advised to ensure the true nature of the spirit.

- ◈ The group emphasizes the importance of respecting negative energies and avoiding unnecessary interactions, as well as the need for discipline and understanding of one's own limits in the paranormal field.

- ◈ The experiences shared by the investigators highlight the diverse and often intense encounters they have had with the paranormal, shaping their beliefs and approaches to their work.

CONTACT - Episode 3

Summary

The video script is about a conversation between two hosts discussing the CE5 protocols and strange occurrences during their live stream. They also mention a upcoming guest and technical issues they are facing.

Description

Christopher Moule and Dakota Frandsen join forces to bring you, "The Bald and Bonkers," where an unfiltered view into worlds known and unknown is brought to you with amazing guests and more! CONTACT is the show dedicated strictly to the UFO Disclosure Movements and more! You never quite know what will happen! Want to know where you can catch Bald and Bonkers? Check out this link: https://www.flowcode.com/page/baldandbonkers

Key Insights

- The hosts are planning changes for their channel, including a new name and trailer. They emphasize the importance of consistency and keeping the channel's branding intact. [⚘]

- The hosts share humorous personal anecdotes to engage the audience and create a light-hearted atmosphere during the discussion. This helps to build rapport and connection. [😄]

- The CE5 protocols and related events are significant topics of conversation, indicating the hosts' interest in UFOs and extraterrestrial encounters. This can attract a specific audience who shares similar interests. [⯑]

- The mention of the CE5 app and night vision goggles highlights the hosts' exploration of different tools and technologies related to UFO investigations. This demonstrates their dedication to the subject matter and their willingness to experiment. [⯑]

- The sudden technical issues during the live stream, including EMF meter spikes, create intrigue and add a sense of mystery to the discussion. This can capture the audience's attention and make them curious about the supernatural or unexplained phenomena. [⯑]

- The hosts refer to recent FBI document releases, suggesting their interest in credible sources and up-to-date information. This adds credibility to their discussion and shows a commitment to providing accurate and relevant content. [⯑]

- Teasing a guest for the next episode and mentioning the success of a previous guest builds anticipation and excitement for future episodes. It also showcases the hosts' ability to attract notable guests, which can enhance the credibility and popularity of their show. [⯑]

Bald and Bonkers - Episode 4

Summary

The video script discusses Elena's experiences with UFOs and ETs, her connection to the Galactic Federation, and the importance of personal empowerment and eliminating fear. There is also speculation about a potential fake alien invasion and the concept of the Earth ascending.

Description

This week's guest: Social Media Influencer Cassius as well ET contactee and author Elena Danaan! Christopher Moule and Dakota Frandsen join forces to bring you, "The Bald and Bonkers," where an unfiltered view into worlds known and unknown is brought to you with amazing guests and more! Attention: This show is designed to create a neutral environment for open discussions on all sorts of topics, paranormal and normal. As such some topics may be offensive to some viewers, so please if you feel you might be offended please do move on. Be sure to subscribe to the channel, hit the notification bell, as this will not only be aired on YouTube but be shared across anywhere you get your podcasts! Join the show live to maybe even join in on the fun and have your questions answered LIVE.

Key Insights

- ⍰ The Galactic Federation and ongoing contact with

benevolent ETs are central to Elena's experiences, highlighting the existence of other life forms in the universe.

- ◈ Personal empowerment and meditation are emphasized as tools to reconnect with one's true self and tap into inherent knowledge.
- ◈ The idea of the Earth ascending and disconnecting from an illusionary matrix suggests a shift in consciousness and a potential transformation of the planet.
- ◈ The possibility of a fake alien invasion is discussed, highlighting the need to discern fear-based messages and maintain individual sovereignty.
- ◈ Seeking knowledge from various sources and trusting one's own intuition is advised in the journey of consciousness.
- ◈ The concept of the universe having breathing cycles aligns with the idea of expansion and contraction, suggesting a cyclical nature of existence.
- ◈ Elena's leisure activities involve reading, connecting with nature, and occasionally watching movies with a conscious perspective.

Bald and Bonkers: CONTACT - Episode 6 - The End is Near?

Summary

-REDACTED-, a paranormal investigator, shares her experiences with extraterrestrial encounters, including out-of-body experiences, encounters with tall figures, and visions of spaceships and symbols. She discusses the difficulty of discussing these experiences and the potential implications for humanity.

Description

On today's show: More Media Coverage tickles the imaginations and speculations of UFO hunters all around! Christopher Moule and Dakota Frandsen join forces to bring you, "The Bald and Bonkers," where an unfiltered view into worlds known and unknown is brought to you with amazing guests and more! CONTACT is our push to talk more of the UFO phenomenon as it is a hot topic with ever increasing activity. Attention: This show is designed to create a neutral environment for open discussions on all sorts of topics, paranormal and normal. As such some topics may be offensive to some viewers, so please if you feel you might be offended please do move on.

Key Insights

- ◈ -REDACTED-'s experiences highlight the complex

and mysterious nature of encounters with extraterrestrial beings, including out-of-body experiences and visions of otherworldly objects and symbols.

- 🔮 The recurring theme of water and underwater machines suggests a connection between extraterrestrial activity and aquatic environments.

- 🔮 The symbols drawn by -REDACTED- may hold significant meaning, potentially representing a star system, a stargate, or a form of extraterrestrial communication.

- 🔮 -REDACTED-'s trust and comfort with the beings she encounters indicate a unique and personal connection that goes beyond conventional understanding.

- 🔮 The potential interest from the government raises questions about the secrecy and control surrounding extraterrestrial encounters and the possible implications for individuals who share their experiences.

- 🔮 -REDACTED-'s distressing encounter during the live stream highlights the potential risks and dangers associated with discussing and delving into extraterrestrial phenomena.

- ⚠ The emotional and physical impact of these experiences on -REDACTED- underscores the need for support, understanding, and further exploration of the extraterrestrial phenomenon.

Bald and Bonkers - Episode 5 - Watch the Lunar Eclipse

Summary

In this YouTube video script, the hosts discuss their experiences with spirits, including encounters with demons and possible extraterrestrial beings. They also talk about their abilities as mediums and how they help spirits cross over to the other side.

Description

On today's show: -REDACTED- Christopher Moule and Dakota Frandsen join forces to bring you, "The Bald and Bonkers," where an unfiltered view into worlds known and unknown is brought to you with amazing guests and more! Attention: This show is designed to create a neutral environment for open discussions on all sorts of topics, paranormal and normal. As such some topics may be offensive to some viewers, so please if you feel you might be offended please do move on.

Key Insights

- ◈ The hosts and guests have had various encounters with spirits, including seeing them, communicating with them, and feeling their presence. This includes experiences with both benevolent and malevolent spirits.

- ◈ They also discuss the existence of extraterrestrial

beings and the possibility that they are already living among us, taking on human form to blend in.

- ◈ -REDACTED- have the ability to help spirits cross over by communicating with them and providing guidance. They also use tools like the Necrophonic app to connect with spirits and receive messages.

- ◈ Pet spirits are a common occurrence for -REDACTED-, with examples of animals appearing as spirits and interacting with them.

- ◈ The hosts and guests believe in the power of collective energy, as their abilities and experiences are strengthened when they come together. They feel a strong connection with each other and with the spirits they encounter.

Bald and Bonkers - Episode 7 - -REDACTED-

Summary

-REDACTED- discusses his experiences in the paranormal field, his YouTube channel -REDACTED- and his social media platform -REDACTED-

Description

On today's show: -REDACTED- of -REDACTED- Christopher Moule and Dakota Frandsen join forces to bring you, "The Bald and Bonkers," where an unfiltered view into worlds known and unknown is brought to you with amazing guests and more! Attention: This show is designed to create a neutral environment for open discussions on all sorts of topics, paranormal and normal. As such some topics may be offensive to some viewers, so please if you feel you might be offended please do move on.

Key Insights

- ◈ -REDACTED- experiences in the paranormal field have led him to create his YouTube channel -REDACTED- and his social media platform -REDACTED-.

- ◈ -REDACTED- is a social media site dedicated to all things paranormal, providing a drama-free platform for enthusiasts to connect and share their experiences.

- 😱 -REDACTED- has had some terrifying experiences

during paranormal investigations, including being choked in a hair salon and feeling a hand on his throat.

- ⯑ -REDACTED- bucket list locations for investigations include Suicide Forest, Tranquil Sanatorium, and the Dead City near Cairo, Egypt.

Bald and Bonkers CONTACT - Episode 7 - Cristina Gomez

Summary

Cristina Gomez, a UFO researcher, shares her journey into the world of UFOs and her personal sighting in India. She emphasizes the importance of remaining humble and critical when researching UFOs and advises starting with historical evidence before delving into personal experiences. She also discusses the potential impact of UFO disclosure on society and the challenges of distinguishing between real UFO sightings and hoaxes or misinterpretations.

Description

On today's show: The Bald and Bonkers Boys are happy to finally get to meet Cristina Gomez; Producer/Presenter at DEBRIEFED and Content Creator at THE PARADIGM SHIFTS https://beacons.page/cristinagomez Christopher Moule and Dakota Frandsen join forces to bring you, "The Bald and Bonkers," where an unfiltered view into worlds known and unknown is brought to you with amazing guests and more! Attention: This show is designed to create a neutral environment for open discussions on all sorts of topics, paranormal and normal. As such some topics may be offensive to some viewers, so please if you feel you might be offended please do move on.

Key Insights

- ◈ The personal UFO sighting experience in India had a profound impact on Cristina Gomez's interest in the UFO phenomenon, but she remains humble and critical in her research.
- ◈ It is crucial to approach UFO research with skepticism and avoid blindly believing everything found on YouTube or other platforms.
- ◈ The recent disclosure of UFO-related information by the Pentagon has brought more attention to the UFO phenomenon, but it is challenging to determine the veracity of sightings amidst hoaxes and misinterpretations.
- ◈ The acceptance of UFO phenomena is gradually increasing, and it is essential to stay open-minded and explore the topic without preconceived notions.
- ◈ Historical evidence serves as a solid foundation for UFO research and can provide valuable insights into the phenomenon.
- ◈ Cristina Gomez's enthusiasm and excitement about the topic are evident throughout the interview, making her a passionate and engaging guest.
- ◈ Cristina Gomez's background in watching "The Twilight Zone" and her father's influence played a significant role in shaping her interest in the UFO phenomenon.

Bald and Bonkers - Episode 8

Summary

In this episode of Bald and Bonkers, the hosts discuss UFO sightings, censorship, and the CE5 protocols. They also share footage of a possible UFO encounter and play tones associated with contact. A viewer named -REDACTED- is mentioned and there are indications of a potential connection to extraterrestrial beings.

Description

On today's show: Bald and Bonkers examines footage from a woman in Canada who believes she captured potential UAP activity. Christopher Moule and Dakota Frandsen join forces to bring you, "The Bald and Bonkers," where an unfiltered view into worlds known and unknown is brought to you with amazing guests and more!

Key Insights

◈ The hosts play tones associated with the CE5 (Close Encounters of the Fifth Kind) protocols, which are said to facilitate communication with extraterrestrial beings. They discuss their experiences and the effects of the tones, including a feeling of being watched and strange audio phenomena. They also mention the importance of being open-minded and fearless in order to establish contact.

◈ The hosts recount a viewer's experience of capturing

footage of unidentified lights in the sky. They analyze the video and speculate on the nature of the objects, ruling out drones or conventional aircraft due to their movements and lack of continuous lights. They suggest further investigation and experimentation to gather more evidence.

� The conversation shifts to the potential existence of life on other planets and the idea that the government may be hiding evidence of extraterrestrial life. They discuss the possibility of a forthcoming disclosure and the role of NASA in gradually revealing information to the public. The hosts express their belief in the existence of other life forms and the vastness of the universe.

� The hosts discuss the power of media and its ability to shape public perception. They highlight examples of product placement influencing consumer behavior and draw parallels to the manipulation of information regarding UFOs and paranormal phenomena. They question the motives behind censorship and the control exerted by those in power.

� The conversation touches on the power of collective consciousness and the potential for humanity to unite in the face of extraterrestrial contact. The hosts emphasize the need for open-mindedness, understanding, and respect in order to navigate the complexities of the UFO phenomenon. They encourage viewers to stay informed, share information, and be open to new possibilities.

? The hosts experience technical difficulties during the live stream, including distorted audio, glitches, and an unexpected removal of a viewer from the chat. They speculate that these issues may be caused by external forces or interference. They express curiosity about the nature of these phenomena and the potential involvement of higher powers.

Follow-up

The video script discusses the urgency of preparing for something big that is coming, possibly related to UFOs. The host encourages viewers to share their experiences and footage. Changes are coming to the show, and the host mentions potential attempts to silence the population. It is emphasized that kindness and love should also strengthen us to fight when necessary.

Bald and Bonkers CONTACT - Episode 8

Summary

The video script discusses various topics, including conspiracy theories, the impact of technology, and the manipulation of information on social media. It emphasizes the importance of critical thinking and the need to question the authenticity of content on the internet.

Description

On today's show: Christopher Moule and Dakota Frandsen join forces to bring you, "The Bald and Bonkers," where an unfiltered view into worlds known and unknown is brought to you with amazing guests and more! Attention: This show is designed to create a neutral environment for open discussions on all sorts of topics, paranormal and normal. As such some topics may be offensive to some viewers, so please if you feel you might be offended please do move on. Be sure to subscribe to the channel, hit the notification bell, as this will not only be aired on YouTube but be shared across anywhere you get your podcasts! Join the show live to maybe even join in on the fun and have your questions answered LIVE.

Key Insights

- ◈ The internet has revolutionized the way we access information, but it has also become a breeding ground for conspiracy theories and fake news. It is crucial to question the authenticity and credibility of the content we encounter online.

- ⟐ Social media platforms like Facebook are designed to be addictive, keeping users engaged and generating more ad revenue. This addictive nature often leads to conflicts and fights among users, amplifying the negative impact of these platforms.

- ⟐ TV shows that focus on paranormal phenomena, such as "Ghost Adventures," often exaggerate and fabricate experiences for entertainment purposes. Viewers should approach these shows with skepticism and seek out more credible sources for paranormal investigations.

- ⟐ The existence of underground bases and alien life on Earth is a popular topic, but credible evidence to support these claims is lacking. While it is intriguing to speculate about the possibility, it is important to approach such claims with critical thinking and skepticism.

- ⟐ Governments have a history of manipulating information for their own agendas, but individuals also manipulate themselves by falling into groupthink and easily accepting misinformation. It is important to think critically, question sources, and seek out reliable information before forming opinions.

Bald and Bonkers - Episode 9 - Iron City Paranormal

Summary

A video script expert shares a YouTube video script for an episode of "Bald and Bonkers" featuring Iron City Paranormal. The script includes discussions about paranormal investigations, historical locations, and captures of potential paranormal activity.

Description

On today's show: Derrick Smith & Daniel Metelsky, co-founders of Iron City Paranormal Investigators. Our team is based out of the Iron City, Pittsburgh, PA. https://ironcity-paranormal.com/ Christopher Moule and Dakota Frandsen join forces to bring you, "The Bald and Bonkers," where an unfiltered view into worlds known and unknown is brought to you with amazing guests and more! Attention: This show is designed to create a neutral environment for open discussions on all sorts of topics, paranormal and normal. As such some topics may be offensive to some viewers, so please if you feel you might be offended please do move on.

Key Insights

- [00:00] ◈ Iron City Paranormal and "Bald and Bonkers" explore historical locations in Pittsburgh, capturing potential paranormal activity.

- [06:30] ⯑ The McGill House investigation reveals a figure walking through a door, potentially a manifestation of a dominant voice heard during the investigation.

- [12:45] ⯑ The Gettysburg EVP captures the sound of a march and flutes, potentially linked to the historical significance of the location.

- [17:10] ⯑ The North Country Brewery investigation captures a figure walking through a doorway, potentially connected to the history of the building as a former residence and funeral home.

- [21:20] ⯑ The Anchorage Mansion picture shows possible transparent faces in a window, aligning with reported experiences and the history of the location.

- [25:35] ⯑ The Blennerhassett Island picture may depict a Native American watcher figure, potentially connected to the history of the island and Native American deaths.

Bald and Bonkers CONTACT - Episode 9

Summary

The video script discusses various topics including strange weather, UFO sightings, social media censorship, and the current state of society. The hosts express their opinions on government, the royal family, and the need for real people to be in power.

Description

On today's show: Secret Facilities Christopher Moule and Dakota Frandsen join forces to bring you, "The Bald and Bonkers," where an unfiltered view into worlds known and unknown is brought to you with amazing guests and more! Attention: This show is designed to create a neutral environment for open discussions on all sorts of topics, paranormal and normal. As such some topics may be offensive to some viewers, so please if you feel you might be offended please do move on.

Key Insights

- [⯑] The hosts discuss the strange and unpredictable weather patterns, which they attribute to climate change and human impact on the planet. This highlights the need for environmental awareness and action.

- [⯑] The conversation touches on the topic of UFO sightings and underground bases, suggesting that there may be hidden extraterrestrial activity around the world. This sparks curiosity about the existence of alien life and the possibility of government cover-ups.

- [◈] The hosts express their frustration with social media censorship and the lack of effective spam filters. They discuss the biased nature of fact-checkers and the restriction of freedom of speech, leading to a sense of disillusionment with the current online platforms.

- [◈] The discussion delves into the current state of society, highlighting the loss of respect, the breakdown of traditional roles, and the increasing division among people. There is a yearning for a return to a time when people were more understanding and connected.

- [◈] The hosts announce an upcoming Christmas show and open panel, where they invite guests to share their paranormal experiences and stories. This reflects their desire to create a community and provide a platform for others to share their interests and beliefs.

- [◈] The conversation explores various theories and locations related to aliens and secret bunkers, such as Wright-Patterson and Denver International Airport. This reveals the hosts' interest in the unknown and their willingness to question established narratives.

Bald and Bonkers - Episode 10

Summary

The YouTube video script discusses various topics related to Christmas and the paranormal. The hosts talk about their personal beliefs and traditions during Christmas, as well as the potential connection between spirits and aliens. They also mention the upcoming new year and the possibility of a new show. The conversation touches on the importance of family, love, and gratitude during the holiday season.

Description

On today's show: Christmas Episode Christopher Moule and Dakota Frandsen join forces to bring you, "The Bald and Bonkers," where an unfiltered view into worlds known and unknown is brought to you with amazing guests and more! Attention: This show is designed to create a neutral environment for open discussions on all sorts of topics, paranormal and normal. As such some topics may be offensive to some viewers, so please if you feel you might be offended please do move on.

Key Insights

- ◈ Christmas is a time for celebrating family, love, and gratitude. It's not just about material gifts, but about being together and showing kindness to others.

- ◈ The hosts speculate on the potential connection

between spirits and aliens, suggesting that they may exist in the same realms or dimensions.

- ♢ The hosts plan a new show for the new year, involving -REDACTED- The details are kept secret, creating anticipation among viewers.

- ♢ The hosts encourage viewers to support each other's channels and help them grow. They emphasize the importance of community and collaboration on YouTube.

- ♢ The hosts announce a competition and express their excitement about reaching a milestone of 1,000 subscribers. They hope to see -REDACTED- channel reach 1,000 subscribers as well.

- ♢ The hosts embrace their baldness and make lighthearted jokes about their appearance. They create a fun and lighthearted atmosphere throughout the episode.

- ♢♢ The hosts use music and laughter to set the tone for the episode, creating an entertaining and festive atmosphere for viewers.

Bald and Bonkers: Contact - Episode 10

Summary

Dakota and Christopher discuss various topics including Krampus, CIA documents, and the abundance of UFO sightings. They also mention upcoming guests and plans for the future of their show.

Description

On today's show: Krampus and the Holiday Spirit Nat NW's New Book: https://amzn.to/3yRgAbg Christopher Moule and Dakota Frandsen join forces to bring you, "The Bald and Bonkers," where an unfiltered view into worlds known and unknown is brought to you with amazing guests and more! Attention: This show is designed to create a neutral environment for open discussions on all sorts of topics, paranormal and normal. As such some topics may be offensive to some viewers, so please if you feel you might be offended please do move on.

Key Insights

- ◈ Christmas spirit: The hosts acknowledge the holiday season and express their excitement for the upcoming celebrations.

- 😈 Krampus folklore: Dakota and Crisper discuss the history and traditions surrounding the figure of Krampus, highlighting the terrifying nature of the character.

- ◈ UFO crash and CIA documents: The hosts mention

the alleged UFO crash and the CIA documents related to the incident, emphasizing the mysterious nature of the event and the survival of only two individuals.

- ⟐ Future plans for the show: Dakota and Christopher mention their upcoming guests and their plans to expand their content in the future, showing their dedication to providing interesting and diverse topics for their audience.

Bald and Bonkers: Contact - Episode 11

Summary

The episode discusses the concept of the multiverse and its implications for extraterrestrial life. It explores the idea that there are multiple dimensions and realities, and that beings from these dimensions may have made contact with Earth. The text also mentions the Mandela Effect and the possibility of parallel universes merging. Overall, it highlights the complexity and infinite possibilities of the multiverse.

Description

On today's show: "Multiverse of Madness" The guys bring you information on the multiverse and potential proof of its existence through evidence found in their investigations. The Last Official Show of 2021 will also be a celebration of making it to 1k on the officialVald and Bonkers YouTube channel! Christopher Moule and Dakota Frandsen join forces to bring you, "The Bald and Bonkers," where an unfiltered view into worlds known and unknown is brought to you with amazing guests and more! Attention: This show is designed to create a neutral environment for open discussions on all sorts of topics, paranormal and normal. As such some topics may be offensive to some viewers, so please if you feel you might be offended please do move on.

Key Insights

- ◈ The concept of the multiverse raises questions about

the nature of reality and the existence of other dimensions and beings. It challenges our understanding of the universe.

- ⟐ The multiverse provides a possible explanation for phenomena like the Mandela Effect, where alternate realities merge and create different memories and experiences.
- ⟐ The existence of extraterrestrial life and contact with other beings is a topic that has been explored and debated for many years. The government's knowledge and preparation for disclosure indicate that contact may have already occurred.
- ⟐ The exploration of the multiverse and the search for extraterrestrial life require a multidisciplinary approach, combining scientific knowledge, technological advancements, and open-mindedness.
- ⟐ The search for extraterrestrial life and contact with other beings can potentially have profound implications for humanity, leading to new perspectives and advancements in technology and understanding.
- ⟐ Organizations like NASA play a crucial role in space exploration and the search for extraterrestrial life. Their efforts and discoveries contribute to our understanding of the universe and potential contact with other civilizations.
- ⟐ The multiverse concept and the possibility of contact with extraterrestrial beings raise philosophical and existential questions about our place in the universe and the nature of life itself.

Contact by Bald and Bonkers - Ep 1

Summary

The video script discusses the belief that aliens exist and have been in contact with Earth for many years. It also highlights the manipulation and censorship by social media platforms and the potential hidden knowledge about civilizations and technology in places like Antarctica and Egypt.

Description

On today's show: "2022 News" A New Year is upon us! What sorts of insanity comes this way? Christopher Moule and Dakota Frandsen join forces to bring you, "The Bald and Bonkers," where an unfiltered view into worlds known and unknown is brought to you with amazing guests and more! Attention: This show is designed to create a neutral environment for open discussions on all sorts of topics, paranormal and normal. As such some topics may be offensive to some viewers, so please if you feel you might be offended please do move on.

Key Insights

- ⟐ The belief in extraterrestrial life and their contact with Earth has been a topic of fascination and debate for many years, sparking discussions about the true nature of our existence in the universe.

- ⟐ Social media platforms like Facebook and YouTube have been accused of manipulating and censoring content, leading to the promotion of fake news and hindering the spread of genuine information.

- ◈ Ancient civilizations like Egypt and potential hidden knowledge in places like Antarctica continue to intrigue researchers and enthusiasts, raising questions about advanced technologies and the possibility of contact with extraterrestrial beings.

Bald and Bonkers - Episode 13

Summary

The video script is about a YouTube show called "Bald and Bonkers" where the hosts discuss strange and paranormal topics. They also mention upcoming episodes and shout out other channels in the community.

Description

Bald and Bonkers - Episode 13 On today's show: "Let's Show Off The Little Guy" Much to the surprise of the hosts, Bald and Bonkers is doing surprisingly well and growing rapidly! Because of this, we wanted to save a spot once a month to geive our friends a chance to promote their stuff. Whether it is your channel, a book, movie, WHATEVER! We want to give you the spotlight!

Key Insights

- � The hosts are excited to announce that "Bald and Bonkers" will be included in a time capsule sent to the moon, giving them an immortal legacy in space.

- � The hosts discuss the importance of supporting each other within the YouTube community and encourage viewers to subscribe to other channels.

- �♀ The upcoming show with Drew on witchcraft and magic aims to provide insights and guidance for viewers interested in exploring their spirituality.

- � The hosts give shout outs to other channels, promoting

collaboration and community growth.

- 🔮 Guests from the Lizzie Borden House and Smith Family Paranormal will be featured in upcoming episodes, bringing unique stories and experiences to the show.

- 🔮 The hosts acknowledge the recent decline in YouTube engagement and encourage viewers to share the video and support the channel.

- 😂 The hosts maintain a lighthearted and humorous tone throughout the video, creating an entertaining and engaging atmosphere for viewers.

Contact by Bald and Bonkers - Ep 2

Summary

The video script discusses the belief that mankind is not alone in the universe and that contact with extraterrestrial beings has already occurred. It focuses on the mysterious activity around Mount Shasta and the potential for future UFO events. The script also mentions the use of tones for communication with advanced civilizations and upcoming projects in the UFO community.

Description

On today's show: "ET Contact and Mt Shasta" Recent efforts in the Bald and Bonkers Boys research indicates that there may be a bit event coming soon at Mt. Shasta in the US involving UFO contact... so let's discuss!

Key Insights

- ◈ Extraterrestrial contact: The script asserts that mankind is not alone in the universe and that contact with extraterrestrial beings has occurred. This belief is based on reported sightings, military reports, and knowledge held by governments for years.

- ◈ Mount Shasta: The mountain is highlighted as a hotbed of UFO activity, with reports of mysterious lights, electronics malfunctioning, and claims of a city of light beneath the mountain. It is considered a significant location for potential future UFO events.

- ◈ Preparation for revelation: The script mentions that governments have been slowly preparing the public for the revelation that we are not alone in the universe. This implies that there may be plans to disclose information about extraterrestrial contact in the future.

- ◈ Different types of extraterrestrials: The existence of different types of extraterrestrial beings is acknowledged, with caution advised in judging them. The script mentions the possibility of some being beneficial and others being clone species with intentions of enslavement.

- ◈ Tones for communication: The use of tones for communication with advanced civilizations is discussed, suggesting that traditional radio transmissions may not be the most effective means of contact. Tones are seen as a potential method for initiating communication with extraterrestrial beings.

- ◈ Investigating Mount Shasta: There are plans to investigate the mysterious activity around Mount Shasta, potentially through hiking or helicopter exploration. The script suggests that something significant may occur at the location within the next few years.

Bald and Bonkers - Episode 14

Summary

The video script discusses the belief that mankind is not alone in the universe and that contact with extraterrestrial beings has already occurred. It focuses on the mysterious activity around Mount Shasta and the potential for future UFO events. The script also mentions the use of tones for communication with advanced civilizations and upcoming projects in the UFO community.

Description

Bald and Bonkers - Episode 14 On today's show: "Axe Away! Stories from the Lizzie Borden House!" The Bald and Bonkers Boys interview a very special guest who worked as a tour guide in the Lizzie Borden House! Come ask your burning questions!

Key Insights

- ⟐ The Lizzie Borden house is believed to be haunted, with multiple spirits present, including Mr. and Mrs. Borden and the spirits of the two drowned children.

- ⟐ The Fall River Historical Society is a valuable resource for learning more about the Borden family and their personal preferences and history.

- ⟐ Colleen believes that Lizzie Borden may have been complicit in the murders, but not the actual killer. She theorizes that Lizzie's uncle, John Morse, may have been involved.

- ⍰ Mr. Borden was a teetotaler and did not allow alcohol in the house, even in modern times during overnight investigations. This strict policy may contribute to the negative energy in the house.

Contact by Bald and Bonkers - Episode 3

Summary

Humanity is not alone in the universe. There are numerous alien races that have made contact with Earth. Some believe that humans have been genetically modified by aliens. There is also speculation about the moon and Mars being bases for alien civilizations. There are different theories about the origin of humans, including being descendants of aliens or being genetically created to live on Earth.

Description

On today's show: "CONTACT! Life as a UFO Contactee" The Bald and Bonkers Boys are no strangers to the unexplainable, but what would life be like being in direct contact with potential ET beings? That's what the guys would like to discuss! Christopher Moule and Dakota Frandsen join forces to bring you, "The Bald and Bonkers," where an unfiltered view into worlds known and unknown is brought to you with amazing guests and more!

Key Insights

- ⍰ The existence of numerous alien races suggests that the universe is teeming with life and that humans are not the only intelligent species.

- ⍰ The moon and Mars have long been subjects of speculation regarding potential bases for alien civilizations, with reports of underground civilizations and unusual anomalies.

- ◈ There are theories that humans may have been genetically modified by aliens, possibly explaining our different races and characteristics.

- ◈ The origin of humans is a topic of debate, with theories ranging from being descendants of aliens to being genetically created to live on Earth.

- ◈ Humans may be on the brink of a significant breakthrough in their understanding and interaction with alien life.

- ◈ The potential future of humanity might involve exploration of other planets and systems, as humans may need to leave Earth to survive and thrive.

- ◈ The existence of aliens and their impact on human history and development is a complex and fascinating subject that continues to spark curiosity and speculation.

Bald and Bonkers - Episode 15

Summary

The video script is about an episode of the YouTube show "Bald and Bonkers" featuring Chad and Linda from Smith Paranormal. They discuss their experiences with the paranormal, including encounters with spirits and UFOs. They also talk about upcoming investigations and merchandise available for purchase.

Description

Bald and Bonkers - Episode 15 On today's show: "Smith Family Paranormal"

Key Insights

◈ Chad and Linda from Smith Paranormal are the guests on the show, discussing their experiences with the paranormal.

◈ Linda shares her first encounter with an apparition, her grandfather, when she was a young girl.

◈ Chad discusses his ability to sense and feel spiritual energy, particularly in historical locations.

◈ Chad also shares his encounter with a UFO while driving, where a bright light followed him through the woods.

◈ Smith Paranormal offers a variety of merchandise, including t-shirts, keychains, and coasters, with their logo and designs related to the paranormal.

Contact by Bald and Bonkers - Episode 4 - Special Philip Mantle Interview

Summary

Mankind has wondered if we are alone in the universe, and now it is confirmed that we are not. The government has known about contact with extraterrestrial beings for years. Philip Mantle, a UFO researcher, shares his experiences and insights into the field.

Description

Contact by Bald and Bonkers - Episode 4 - Special Philip Mantle Interview On today's show: "Philip Mantle" The Bald and Bonkers Boys meet UFOlogist Philip Mantle to discuss his history and learn more about how to take on the field as it is continuing to blow up. What will the guys uncover? Flying Disk Press: https://flyingdiskpress.blogspot.com/ Christopher Moule and Dakota Frandsen join forces to bring you, "The Bald and Bonkers," where an unfiltered view into worlds known and unknown is brought to you with amazing guests and more!

Key Insights

- ◈ The government's confirmation of contact with extraterrestrial beings validates years of speculation and reports.

- ◈ Philip Mantle's personal experiences and involvement in UFO research lend credibility to his insights.

- ◈ The vastness of the universe presents challenges in the search for other intelligent life forms.

- ◈ The released videos by the US Navy provide visual evidence of unidentified aerial phenomena.

- ◈ UFO research requires a balanced approach of skepticism and open-mindedness.

- ◈ The UFO field offers opportunities for exploration, learning, and meeting people from various backgrounds.

- ◈ The search for answers in the UFO field continues, with many unanswered questions and ongoing investigations.

Bald and Bonkers - Episode 16

Summary

The hosts discuss their personal experiences with UFOs and spiritual encounters, emphasizing the importance of meditation and spiritual growth. They also mention the upcoming documentary on UFOs and the potential for disclosure in the future.

Description

Bald and Bonkers - Episode 16 On today's show: "The Chad Smith Podcast" The guys have Chad Smith come on to help promote his show and discuss all things strange.

Key Insights

- ◈♂ Meditation and spiritual practices are crucial for connecting with higher dimensions and understanding the true nature of reality.
- ◈ UFO sightings and encounters are diverse, with different beings appearing in various forms and frequencies.
- ◈ The orbs seen and others are likely spiritual beings, and their increasing activity indicates a desire for disclosure.
- ◈ The spiritual realm transcends traditional human labels and terminology, requiring an open mind to fully grasp its complexity.
- ◈ The hosts believe that disclosure and humanity's spiritual awakening could lead to a more peaceful and united world.

- ⯑ Personal experiences with spiritual encounters vary, with some individuals having direct communication with entities and receiving guidance.

- ⯑ The presence of orbs over the ocean suggests that beings may be living underwater, expanding the possibilities of otherworldly life.

www.ingramcontent.com/pod-product-compliance
Lightning Source LLC
LaVergne TN
LVHW040516210926
848480LV00005BA/1481
9798869122353